i reveal to the therapist

by Lori A Minor

Cover art by Lori A Minor

Cover poem and photo published as haiga in
issue 24 of Failed Haiku.

To anyone suffering from mental illness.
Keep fighting the good fight;

Introduction

Age 9:   Begins therapy and meds.
Age 10:   Stops all treatment.
Age 12:   Second dose of therapy, med
            changes.
Age 14:   Suicide attempt, inpatient, med
            changes.
Age 14:   Agrees to long term outpatient
            therapy with new therapist, new
            psychiatrist, case worker, and
            mentor.
Age 17:   Med changes.
Age 18:   Patient's decision to stop meds
            and all outpatient programs.
Age 21:   Refuses meds, agrees to individual
            and group therapy.
Age 22:   Agrees to meds.
Age 23:   Stops all treatment.
Age 24:   Suicide attempt, outpatient
            therapy, new meds.
Age 24:   Stops all treatment.
Age 26:   Managing, barely.

signs of depression
the first leaf falls
to my feet

diagnosis
the last leaf
still holding on

asking myself
what it took to get here
the therapist's couch

snapdragon
opening up
about my past

Safe Space

He grounded me for everything.
Whispering at the table. Crying. Wetting
the bed. It wasn't your typical
grounding where you can't play with
friends or you get the PlayStation
cables taken away. I had to live in my
room and the only reason I was allowed
out was to shower, but he insisted on
monitoring me. Said it was to make sure
I wasn't "playing around". Dinner was
served in my room. Sometimes only cheese
and crackers, and if I was lucky, a few
slices of pepperoni. My room became my
safe space. It was the only home I knew
and even now, sixteen years later, I
still find it hard to leave.

voyeurism
even the moon
has eyes

hide and seek
another game
against myself

domestic violence
the cry
of a nestling

damselfly
they all leave me
in distress

stuck on the bottom
of the seesaw
bipolar depression

porcelain doll
I reglue pieces
of myself

emoticon
another way
to fake my smile

Picture Perfect

Sometimes depression makes you think
that your family would be better off
without you. I'm staring at an Easter
photo of my mom, dad, 13 year old
brother, and 11 year old sister and
nothing looks out of place. They're a
beautiful family with no me to be
missed.

childhood puzzle
a few pieces
go missing

white crayon
in all this blue
I have no color

bipolar low
a rainbow fading
into gray skies

freak show

my mom always told me god never makes
mistakes. well, here i am. his one major
design flaw, set on display for all the
world to see.

waxing moon
I settle in
to my bruises

telling me I deserved it winter smog

lake effect
my apology
is not enough

reverting back
to who I was
before mania…
the ebb and flow
of crashing waves

gathering up
all my pieces
after depression
the fog dwindles
into the sea

Barely Breathing

What if I told you that depression is a
big black hole? Like the Bermuda
triangle. It just sucks you in and you
lose yourself in the center of the deep
blue sea. And you're drowning and
there's no one there to save you. No
lifeguard. No rescue boat. And you're
not wearing a life jacket. The only
thing you can do is try to float and
hope that the current takes you to
shore. Just when you think the worst is
over, a wave crashes down on you and
you're sinking again, feeling your lungs
fill up with water and suddenly you're
barely breathing. At this point, all
hope is lost. You just know you're gonna
die… but a miracle happens and you're
floating again. And that's all you can
do. Just keep on floating.

washing ashore
the remains
of a baby shark
the lifeguard looks
in the other direction

Oblivion

I'm twenty-two, depressed, and I hate my life. I haven't checked my final grades because I know I'm failing out of college, not like I can take out more loans anyways, so I take another shot of vodka as my laughter blends in with the crowd.

surrounded
by friends
nobody notices
I'm writing
my suicide note

butterfly effect
I survive
my attempt

cat scratch
another lie
about my scars

desk flowers
this longing
to escape

plucking the petals
until it loses beauty
trichotillomania

autumn lilac
the part of me
that withers away

somewhere between
winter and spring
bipolar disorder

withered iris
she hides
her black eye

fingering the crucifix
she asks forgiveness
for being abused

Divine Intervention

Did you know I'm going to hell? Did you?
Well, you see, I'm a sinner. I live in
sin. I'm consumed by it, but aren't we
all? That's why Jesus died on the cross.
Forgiveness, right? And yet here we are.
I'm going to hell. I'll see you there.

holy water
I drink away
my transgressions

wishing I was just as super moon

             winter trees
             the nakedness
             I try to hide

before the rape
he assures me
it's okay
the beetle chews
through the leaf

the tulip's edges
begin to wither
suicidal thoughts

slow down/speed up

I'm a completely different person when I'm depressed. Bipolar disorder is funny that way. During a manic streak I am a superhero. I can get a thousand things done in one day. The kitchen will be spotless with a full breakfast on the table by 10 AM at the latest and when it comes to editing, I can respond to 60 submissions without a break. Yet, this depression is nasty. It comes so suddenly, without any warning. Before I know it I have a pile of unfinished art pieces. There are stacks of dirty dishes. I'm stuffing my face with endless bags of chips while lying in bed, binge-watching some Seth MacFarlane cartoon I've seen a hundred times just trying to get out a smile.

solar eclipse
I wait out
this darkness

showering
for the first time
in weeks
I scrub off what's left
of my depression

reaching
the seabed
moodswings

dying my hair
a different color
I try
to hide
who I am

convinced I need
to remove
the bad parts of me
I pull another hair
from my scalp

garbage day
gathering up
who I used to be

dissociation
mourning the loss
of who I was

high school never ends

I don't make friends easily. I'm
socially awkward. The entire church was
invited to my Sweet Sixteen and only the
pastor came. It's like people can smell
  the stench of my mental illness from
miles away. Even now I don't get invited
places and no one comes to my art shows
               or gatherings.

              birthday candles
               I try to hide
               my darkness

a shot in the dark

College is about finding out who you
are, right? Well, when I was in college
I was everyone but myself. I desperately
tried to fit in somewhere… anywhere. I
became the center of rumors when all I
wanted was a friend. I tried too hard
and made everyone hate me when in
reality I only just needed to be.

winter chill
searching for
that perfect snowflake

support system
loving me more
when I'm medicated

family dinner
adding salt
to my own wounds

bloody tongue
the taste of words
I refuse to say

professional athlete
throwing punches
at myself

settling down
from a mood swing
the clouds
swiftly move
across the moon

finding myself
as gray as
the sky
sips of bland tea
in the city winter

shock waves

It's three in the morning and the sky is
completely clear, but there are no stars
in sight. The light pollution just
drowns them out. It's almost like
they're dead... and I'm mourning the loss
of each one.

power struggle
the worm curls
into itself

cicada husks
I don't speak up
about the rape

scraping the seawall
I finally learn
to say no

all my thoughts spinning spiderwebs

crippling anxiety
the jitter
of a moth's wings

Lights Out

I'm looking for a lightbulb to go in my
new lamp. 60 watt max. What does that
mean? So there's a 40 watt and an 80
watt. Where's the 60? What if I buy the
40 and that's actually more than 60,
like gauges, the smaller number is
actually bigger. But 80 is clearly more
than 60. I need the 60 watt because if I
buy 80 or 40 I could blow up my lamp.
Which means house fire and if I burn the
house down we lose everything, clothes,
art, laptops— I have poems in there. And
the cat! What if she's in the basement
and we can't get her out and she dies?
I'll kill her and it'll be my fault all
because I bought the wrong lightbulb...

10k race
all of my thoughts
pass each other

dissociation
losing myself
in fun house mirrors

never finding
the gray area
borderline personality

whiteout
my visibility reduces
to sadness

waiting for spring
my sadness lingers
in the last frost

this empty house
immersed in fog
post traumatic dreams

binge eating
the hunger moon
never full

rose-tinted glasses

I am fat because I was told I am fat. I
am ugly because society says that I am.
I am fat and ugly because my beauty is
less than the standard. I can't help but
wonder how I would feel about myself if
the world was taught free thinking
instead of conditioning.

anorexia
I starve myself
of value

the icicle drips
freeze over
social isolation

begging
to touch the sun
agoraphobia

moon craters
illuminating the void
that I created

blamed for the rape
light pollution covers
the stars

identical twins
the sky and I
both gray

longing for more
than this life can give
blue moon

Crash-test

The only time I buy razors is to cut
myself. I used to shave, but you can't
get a high from just grazing your skin.
It's releasing the endorphins that
really make you feel good. Of course,
then I crash and feel guilty about what
I did. Recovery takes a while. I've been
in recovery for twelve years now and
clean for almost seven months.

riding a bike
for the first time
in years
I squeeze the breaks
a little too hard

in my prime
and living longer
than I expected
this mayfly fades
into the light

releasing
the firefly
from my palm
one year free
from self harm

pulling off
the butterfly's wings
trichotillomania

seeing myself
in a new light
luna moth

covered in dust
I remember
how happiness feels

sunbeams touch
the empty room
manic streak

Holes

The most vulnerable pieces of me are
found tucked away in the crevices of my
bedroom. It's the dirty bra tossed in
the closet, the food wrapper pushed
between the mattress and wall, the empty
wine bottle on the dresser, and the
blood-stained panties kicked under the
bookshelf.

old teddy bear
all the wounds
I can't hide

purging
I indulge on
society's ideals

skewed beauty
I decide
what's good enough

erasing the stigma
I clean the dirt
from under my nails

Some poems in this book have appeared in the following publications:

#FemkuMag
Akitsu Quarterly
Blithe Spirit
Contemporary Haibun Online
Failed Haiku
Haiku Commentary
Haikuniverse
Incense Dreams
Living Haiku Anthology
O:JA&L; Open: Journal of Arts & Letters
Prune Juice
Scryptic Magazine
Seashores
Stardust Haiku
The Haiku Foundation's Per Diem
The Haiku Registry
The Zen Space
Under the Basho

Special credits:

"Barely Breathing"
third place winner 2017 Where Tanka Prose
Grows Contest

"family dinner"
third place winner 2017 H. Gene Murtha
Senryu Contest

Lori A Minor is a feminist, existentialist, mental health advocate, and body positive activist who dabbles in both literary and visual arts. Her work tackles issues related to body image, mental health, and social awareness. She is the founder and editor of #FemkuMag and former editor of Scryptic Magazine. In September 2017, Lori published her first book *Radical Women: A Book of Femku*. Her work has appeared in Frogpond, the Michigan State University LookOut! Gallery's Haiga Around the World Exhibit, the season of haiku exhibit at Holden Arboretum, and more. Lori is honored to be the third place winner in the 2017 H Gene Murtha Senryu Contest, as well as in the short list for the 2017 Touchstone Award.